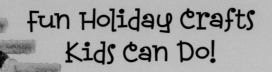

Fun Holiday Crafts
Kids Can Do!

Christmas Crafts

Fay Robinson

Enslow Publishers, Inc.

40 Industrial Road
Box 398
Berkeley Heights, NJ 07922
USA

PO Box 38
Aldershot
Hants GU12 6BP
UK

http://www.enslow.com

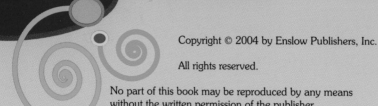

Library of Congress Cataloging-in-Publication Data

Robinson, Fay.
     Christmas crafts / Fay Robinson.
          v. cm. — (Fun holiday crafts kids can do)
     Includes bibliographical references and index.
     Contents: Evergreen bough— Stained glass window—Sock snowman—
Christmas photo frame—Jiggling elves—Christmas village—Santa
sneeze box—Rudolph and the gang—Fuzzy candy canes—3-D table
tree.
     ISBN 0-7660-2257-9 (hardcover : alk. paper)
     1. Christmas decorations--Juvenile literature. [1. Christmas
decorations. 2. Handicraft.] I. Title. II. Series.
TT900.C4R59 2003
745.594'12—dc21

                                        2003002751

Printed in the United States of America

10 9 8 7 6 5 4 3 2 1

To Our Readers: We have done our best to make sure all Internet addresses in this book were
active and appropriate when we went to press. However, the author and the publisher have no
control over and assume no liability for the material available on those Internet sites or on other
Web sites they may link to. Any comments or suggestions can be sent by e-mail to
comments@enslow.com or to the address on the back cover.

Illustration credits: Crafts prepared by Margaret Frase.
                    Photography by Carl Feryok.

Cover Photos: Carl Feryok

Contents

*Safety Note: Be sure to ask for help from an adult, if needed, to complete these crafts!

introduction

It's Christmas! This winter holiday is filled with love and giving. People decorate their homes inside and out. They make and buy gifts for their family. And if children are good . . . Santa visits! Family and friends come together for a big Christmas dinner. It is an exciting and joyful time.

But Just How Did Christmas Get Started?

The story of Christmas comes from the Bible. Long ago, Mary and her husband, Joseph, traveled to the town of Bethlehem. When they got there, they found that there was no room at the inn. They had to stay in a stable. That is where Mary's baby, Jesus Christ, was born. They placed him in a manger, which is a feed box for farm animals.

The story says that a star appeared above the stable.

Three Wise Men followed the star's light to bring gifts for the baby. They honored him because they believed he was the infant King of their people. The Bible says Jesus Christ was the son of God.

Hundreds of years later, many people had become Christians. They believed in Jesus Christ. The Christian leaders decided to celebrate His birthday with a holiday. It was called Christ's Mass, or Christmas.

Christmas is celebrated differently around the world. But for most Christians, Christmas is considered the most important holiday of the year. Today, Christmas is celebrated by decorating trees, singing Christmas carols, sending cards, and showing love for our family and friends.

So make a bunch of bouncing elves. Sneeze with Santa at your side. Put some reindeer on your dresser to keep you company while you wait for Christmas morning. Use the crafts in this book to have the merriest Christmas ever!

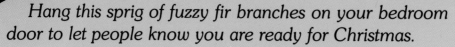

Evergreen Bough

Hang this sprig of fuzzy fir branches on your bedroom door to let people know you are ready for Christmas.

What You Will Need:

- scissors
- 3 green pipe cleaners
- ruler
- 2 brown pipe cleaners
- red ribbon
- bell (optional)

1. To make pine needles, cut three green pipe cleaners into pieces about 2 inches long. Make sure you have eighteen pine needle pieces altogether.

2. Cut two brown pipe cleaners in half for branches.

3. Starting about 2 inches from one end of a branch, twist one pine needle at a time around the branch. Attach six pine needles down the length of the branch. Together, this will make twelve pine needles.

4. Move the pine needles on the branch so they are evenly spaced. Bend the pine needles so they point down. Then, bend the end of the branch up to hold the pine needles in place.

5. Make two more branches with pine needles the same way.

6. Twist the top ends of the branches together. Tie a piece of red ribbon around the branches and make a bow. If you have a bell, attach it to the ribbon.

Gather all your pipe cleaner pieces. . .

Carefully bend them around the stem. . .

Your evergreen bough is ready to be hung!

Holiday Hint:

Ask an adult to attach the evergreen bough to your bedroom door. Now everyone will know you are ready to welcome in the holidays!

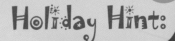

Stained-Glass Window

A stained-glass window will give your home a holiday glow.

What You Will Need:

- pencil
- tracing paper
- ruler
- black crayon
- watercolor paints

- clean, dry plastic foam tray (from the grocery store)
- water
- paintbrush

1. Draw a Christmas design, such as a Christmas tree, on the tracing paper with a pencil. If you like, use the pattern on page 29.

2. Divide the Christmas tree and the background into small, odd-shaped spaces. Use a ruler to draw straight lines.

3. Go over the pencil lines with a black crayon. Press hard and make the black lines thick. These lines will be the "lead" between the "glass" pieces.

4. Mix several shades of green paint on the plastic foam tray. Use different amounts of green, yellow, and blue paints. Be sure to use plenty of water so your colors are watery, not thick.

5. Paint each section of your Christmas tree with a different shade of green. Be careful to paint inside your black lines. Then, paint your background with other colors.

6. Let the paint dry well.

Start by drawing on some tracing paper. . .

Divide the tree and background into small spaces. . .

Your colorful stained-glass window is ready for display!

Holiday Hint:

Tape your design to a sunny window. Watch how the sun shines through for a beautiful Christmas decoration!

Sock Snowman

No snow? Don't worry. You can make a snowman anyway!

What You Will Need:

- cotton balls
- old white tube sock
- scissors
- white yarn or string
- white glue

- small buttons or sequins
- ruler
- orange pipe cleaner
- piece of cloth
- pom-pom (optional)

1. Stuff cotton balls into the sock until it is packed tightly.

2. To make your snowman's head, cut a piece of yarn or string and tie off the top section of the sock. Next, make the middle part by tying off a slightly bigger section. Then, tie off the bottom to make the biggest "snowball."

3. To give your snowman eyes and a mouth, glue on small buttons or sequins.

4. Glue three buttons or sequins down the body.

5. Cut a 1½-inch piece of orange pipe cleaner for the nose. Make a tiny cut below your snowman's eyes. Put some glue on the ends of the pipe cleaner. Push the nose into place and hold it until the glue dries.

6. Cut a long, rectangular strip of cloth to make a scarf. Tie it around the snowman's neck. Then, cut out a wide triangle from the cloth and glue the ends together to make a hat. If you like, add a pom-pom to the hat.

Start by tying off sections for the body. . .

Add the buttons. . .

Next comes the nose. . .

Add the finishing touches. . .

Your snowman is ready to spread Christmas cheer!

Holiday Hint:

Your snowman can keep you company while you wait for Christmas to come. He will stay nice and warm, and you know he will never melt!

Christmas Photo Frame

This is a great gift. Take a picture of someone as he or she opens it. Put the photo inside the frame to save the Christmas memory!

What You Will Need:

- poster board
- ruler
- scissors
- white glue
- Christmas wrapping paper
- clear tape
- ribbons, stickers, glitter, or yarn
- photograph
- construction paper

1. Cut four strips of poster board. Use a ruler to make sure each strip is 2½ inches wide and 11 inches long. Glue them together to make a rectangular shape.

2. Cut a piece of Christmas wrapping paper that is at least 1 inch bigger than your frame. Wrap the frame, covering the opening for now. Tape the ends to the poster board as shown.

3. Poke a hole in the middle with your scissors. Cut four lines in an X-shape out to the corners of the frame. You will have four triangle-shaped flaps.

4. Pull the flaps back one at a time. Cut them so they do not hang over the edge of the frame. Tape them down. Add ribbon, stickers, glitter, or other items to decorate your frame.

5. Glue a photograph in the center of a piece of construction paper. Then, glue the picture and paper to the back of the frame. Make sure your photo is in the center. Cut away any construction paper that is sticking out.

6. Glue some ribbon or yarn to the back of your frame to make it easy to hang.

Wrap christmas paper around the poster board. . .

Carefully cut it to make the middle of your frame. . .

Decorate it and tape a piece of ribbon or yarn to the back . . .

And your frame is ready to display your favorite photo!

Holiday Hint:

If you can't take a picture on christmas day, you can use a photo of yourself, a family member, or pet instead.

Jiggling Elves

Watch Santa's helpers bounce around for Christmas fun.

What You Will Need:

- large pom-poms
- scissors
- colored felt
- white glue
- tiny wiggle eyes
- small pom-poms
- pipe cleaners
- pencil
- egg carton

1. For each elf's head, use one large pom-pom. Cut a triangle out of felt and glue the ends together for a hat. Glue the hat onto the elf's head. If you like, glue the flap down in front, as shown.

2. Glue on a pair of tiny wiggle eyes and a little pom-pom nose.

3. Wind a pipe cleaner around and around a pencil to make a spring. Slide it off. Glue one end of the spring to your elf's head.

4. Cut the egg carton in half and turn it upside down.

5. Stick the loose end of the pipe cleaner into one section of the egg carton. Bend the end of the pipe cleaner from underneath and glue it down. Glue the bottom of the spring to the outside of the egg carton, too.

Glue the hat onto the elf's head. . .

Don't forget to add the eyes and nose. . .

Next is the pipe cleaner spring. . .

You can make shelves of elves!

Holiday Hint:

Make six elves, one for each section of the egg carton. You can make each one different by changing the colors of their hats and noses. Gently shake the egg carton and watch your elves jiggle!

Christmas Village

Put this little village on a tabletop to bring some winter cheer inside!

What You Will Need:

- scissors
- blue, black, and yellow construction paper
- white crayon
- white glue
- silver glitter

1. Cut the blue sheet of construction paper in half.

2. Draw house shapes on the black construction paper with a white crayon. Make different shapes for each house. If you like, you can use the patterns on page 27.

3. To make windows and doors, cut out little squares and rectangles from the yellow paper. One easy way to do this is to make thin strips of paper, then cut off pieces from the end of the strip.

4. Cut out the houses.

5. Glue the windows and doors onto your houses.

6. To put snow on your houses, put some glue on each rooftop. Sprinkle on glitter. Let the glue dry.

7. Fold up the bottom edges of your houses and glue the flaps to the blue paper. Stand your houses up and your Christmas village is complete!

Draw the shapes of the houses and add the windows and doors. . .

Cut out the houses. . .

Take a sheet of black paper. . .

Glue the houses to the blue construction paper. . .

Add some white felt squares for snow and your village is finished!

Holiday Hint:

For a final snowy touch, glue white felt to the blue construction paper, as shown. Now imagine . . . what kind of Christmas fun is going on inside those cozy houses?

17

Santa Sneeze Box

Let Santa help you get over that winter cold!

What You Will Need:

- scissors
- red, black, and yellow construction paper
- square box of tissues
- clear tape
- pencil
- white glue
- white felt

1. To make Santa's jacket, cut a piece of red construction paper and wrap it around the tissue box. Use tape to hold it in place. Cover the top of the tissue box, leaving a slot for the tissues.

2. To make Santa's belt and buckle, cut out the belt from the black construction paper. Cut out the buckle from the yellow construction paper. Glue the buckle to the middle of the belt. Then, glue the belt to the middle of Santa's jacket.

3. Trace and cut out Santa's head, eyes, nose, and mouth. Use the patterns on page 28, if you like. Glue on Santa's face.

4. Trace and cut out the hat on page 28 from the red construction paper. Trace and cut out the tassel on page 28. Glue the tassel to the hat. Then, glue the hat to Santa's head.

5. To make Santa's beard, glue white felt to his chin. If you like, you can also use felt for the tassel and eyebrows.

6. Put some glue on Santa's neck and slide it between the red paper and the tissue box. Let it dry. Pull up the first tissue and your sneeze box is ready to be used.

Cover a tissue box with red paper. . .

Glue on Santa's belt. . .

Next is Santa's head. . .

Glue on the hat and beard. . .

Your Santa Sneeze Box is ready for Christmas!

Holiday Hint:

Pull up a tissue so it looks more like Santa's beard. The next time you sneeze, pretend Santa is sneezing, too!

Rudolph and the Gang

Place these reindeer around your house to bring a Christmas smile to your guests!

What You Will Need:

- tan pipe cleaners (one 5-inch piece and two 4-inch pieces)
- brown pipe cleaner (one 4½-inch piece)
- white glue
- large tan pom-poms
- medium tan pom-poms
- tan felt
- small wiggle eyes
- small red pom-poms
- small black pom-poms
- red or green ribbon

1. Using the 5-inch tan pipe cleaner, start at one end and bend up 1 inch for the tail. Keep 2 inches straight for the body. Bend the other end up 1½ inches for the neck, and bend the last ½ inch down for the head.

2. Bend the 4-inch pieces in half and wrap them around the body sections as shown for the legs.

3. Bend the 4½-inch piece of brown pipe cleaner in half and squeeze it onto the reindeer's head. Squeeze the hoop shut. Bend the antler tips forward.

4. Glue one large tan pom-pom onto each side of the body. Glue one medium tan pom-pom onto each side of the head. (Leave some pipe cleaner for the neck.) Let the pieces dry.

5. Cut ears out of the tan felt and glue them onto the head. Glue on the wiggle eyes and a small pom-pom for a nose (red for Rudolph, black for the other reindeer). Let the pieces dry.

6. Tie a red or green bow around the neck of your reindeer and place it on a table or counter to make people smile!

Start with tan pipe cleaners for the body and brown for the antlers...

Add the pom-poms...

Your reindeer is ready for action!

Holiday Hint:

You can make eight reindeer—plus Rudolph—and arrange them like they are pulling Santa's sleigh. Can you remember the names of all Santa's reindeer?

Fuzzy Candy Canes

You can eat the real ones. These candy canes are for your tree!

What You Will Need:

- red pipe cleaners
- clean, dry plastic foam tray (from the grocery store) or newspaper
- white glue
- white pipe cleaners
- scissors
- ribbon

1. Place two red pipe cleaners side by side on a plastic foam tray or folded newspaper. Run a thin line of glue between them. Hold them together until the glue is dry.

2. To make stripes, wind a white pipe cleaner down the length of the red ones as shown.

3. Carefully use scissors to cut the ends of the pipe cleaners to the same length.

4. Curve the top of the pipe cleaners into a U-shape.

5. Tie a bow around the candy cane with ribbon.

Start with two red pipe cleaners. . .

Carefully twist them with a white one. . .

Finish with a bow, and your candy cane is ready to hang on your Christmas tree!

Holiday Hint:

Make several candy canes. Then, hook them onto your Christmas tree. Or, you can put them in a thin vase like flowers for a fun Christmas decoration.

3-D Table Tree

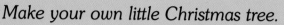

Make your own little Christmas tree.

What You Will Need:

- green and red construction paper
- pencil
- scissors
- cardboard
- ruler
- white glue
- colorful sequins or glitter
- cotton balls

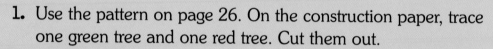

1. Use the pattern on page 26. On the construction paper, trace one green tree and one red tree. Cut them out.

2. Cut up the dotted line to the middle of one tree. Cut down from the top of the other tree to the middle. Slide one tree shape into the other, as shown.

3. Cut a strip of cardboard that is 1½ inches wide and 4 inches long. Roll it up and glue the ends to form the trunk of your tree. Glue the trunk to the center of the remaining cardboard. This will be the base.

4. Slip the tree into the trunk and adjust the sides so that it stands straight up.

5. Glue on sequins or glitter to decorate your tree. Let the glue dry.

6. Glue some cotton balls to the base to look like snow.

Trace the trees on red and green paper. . .

Carefully cut on the dotted lines. . .

Slide one tree shape into the other. . .

Glue the base. . .

Slip the tree into the base. . .

Your Christmas tree is ready to be displayed!

Holiday Hint:

Put your tree on a table or your nightstand. You can even wrap tiny boxes to put underneath it.

Patterns

Use tracing paper to copy the patterns on these pages. Ask an adult to help you cut and trace the shapes onto construction paper.

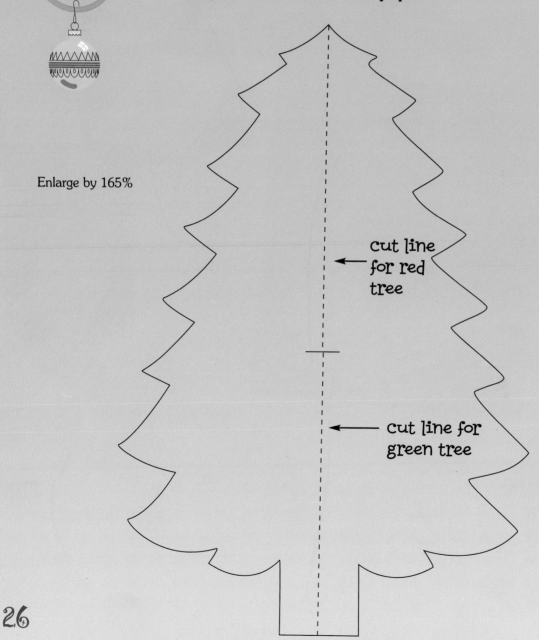

Enlarge by 165%

cut line
for red
tree

cut line for
green tree

At 100%

fold on the dotted line

27

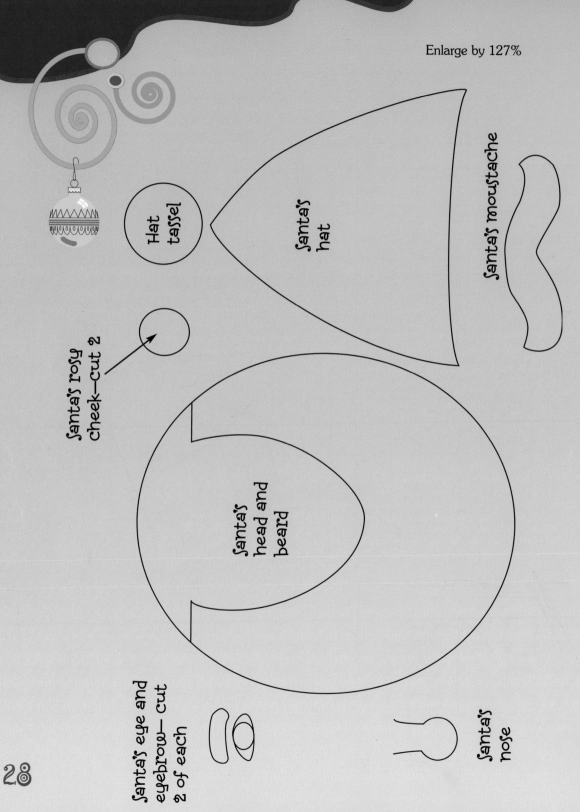

Hat tassel

Santa's hat

Santa's moustache

Santa's rosy cheek—cut 2

Santa's head and beard

Santa's eye and eyebrow— cut 2 of each

Santa's nose

Enlarge by 143%

Reading About Christmas

Cooney, Barbara. *The Story of Christmas*. New York: HarperCollins, 1995.

Erlbach, Arlene. *Christmas—Celebrating Life, Giving, and Kindness*. Berkeley Heights, N.J.: Enslow Publishers, Inc., 2001.

Erlbach, Arlene, and Herbert Erlbach. *Merry Christmas Everywhere*. Brookfield, Conn.: Millbrook, 2002.

Goode, Dianne. *Dianne Goode's Christmas Magic: Poems and Carols*. New York: Random House, 1992.

Moore, Clement. *The Night Before Christmas*. New York: Putnam, 1998.

Roop, Connie and Peter Roop. *Let's Celebrate Christmas*. Brookfield, Conn.: Millbrook, 1997.

Ross, Kathy. *Crafts for Christmas*. Brookfield, Conn.: Millbrook, 1995.

Internet Addresses

A Christmas Celebration

This great Web site provides Christmas gift ideas, songs, recipes, and more.

<http://www.itschristmas.com/index.htm>

Holidays at Kids Domain

Crafts, online games, and stories about Christmas can be found at this fun Web site.

<http://www.kidsdomain.com/holiday/xmas>

31

Index